I0191898

M. Sinclair Allison

Snowflakes and other tales

M. Sinclair Allison

Snowflakes and other tales

ISBN/EAN: 9783741178535

Manufactured in Europe, USA, Canada, Australia, Japa

Cover: Foto ©Andreas Hilbeck / pixelio.de

Manufactured and distributed by brebook publishing software
(www.brebook.com)

M. Sinclair Allison

Snowflakes and other tales

SNOWFLAKES,

AND

OTHER TALES.

BY

M. SINCLAIR ALLISON.

R. WASHBOURNE,
18 PATERNOSTER ROW, LONDON.
1885.

CONTENTS.

SNOWFLAKES.

SNOWFLAKES.

T is Christmas Eve. But not such a Christmas Eve as country children know and love to picture.

The air is not crisp and clear; no fields and meadows are to be seen covered with freshly-fallen snow or sparkling hoar-frost; no trees or hedges hung with glittering icicles. There is no hard-frozen road over which merry feet scamper, as their owners bear along, midst fun and laughter, the holly boughs to deck their home, or the ashen fagot to blaze and crackle upon the large open hearth.

No; the scene of which we are writing is very different, for it is in the heart of a busy city. Omnibuses, carts, and cabs pass and repass in the bustling streets; people jostle and elbow each other as they hurry by on the damp and greasy pavement; while the dull leaden clouds look so close to the tops of the tall sooty chimneys that we feel quite sure that the snowstorm which has been threatening all the day must soon fall now.

Country children would find it very sad and dreary, especially if they chanced to catch sight of a little figure crouching against the iron railings round one of the tallest and gloomiest of the houses. Not a light is to be seen in any of the grimy looking windows. The stone steps, on one of which little Pierre is sitting, and which lead up to a black, sulky looking door, are dirty and uneven; though the busy folks who from morning till evening seem to go incessantly up and down them, are far too intent on the business of the moment to notice this. However, the house is silent and deserted now, for though it is scarcely five o'clock, the eager money-making men have all departed; the heavy sulky door is locked, not to be opened again till the joy-bells have rung out, ' Peace and good-will towards men.' Certainly little Pierre would not recognise these same portly gentlemen, could he see them now in their bright cosy homes, as they toss baby in the air, or stoop down on their big solemn knees to allow little Tom or Lily to rifle their pockets of an endless store of toys and sweetmeats.

How can poor little Pierre picture to himself such a home-scene as this, when his own idea and recollections of one are so widely different? Is he dreaming of *his* home now, I wonder, as, seated on the worn and muddy steps, he leans against the area railings, heedless of the damp and cold? Do you see how one little arm is twined round a bar, and supports his head; how the eyes, which seem so

large and dark in contrast to the thin,
sallow face, have a wistful, far-away
look?

Ah, assuredly little Pierre is thinking of
something very different from the wooden
tray of matches which, hung from his
neck by a leathern strap, rests unnoticed
upon his knees. See how the stream of
foot-passengers continues to flow past him,
yet he never attempts to accost them and
offer his boxes of lights for sale! For
Pierre is no longer in the bustling English
city, but far away in the little village in
Auvergne where the *bonne maman* lives—
the old *bonne maman* who took him and
little Henri and baby Jeanne, when father
and mother died. It is eight months
since he has seen that little French home,
and to one of Pierre's age eight months
is a long long time; but how well he
remembers it all!

The small old-fashioned village with its
one narrow crooked street, which he used

to think so grand, it seemed to lie so
snugly against the big mountain which
sheltered it. How free and happy he had
been in the summer-time, when the sun
shone warm and bright and he ran bare-
footed up the winding mountain-path,
picking gay flowers, and waving grasses
to offer to any chance visitor whom the
coach might bring to the village! How
pleased and proud he had been to bring
the *bonne maman* a few centimes earned
in this way, or by acting as guide to
strangers! But although the centimes
were counted and recounted, they made
very few sous. And then came the long
winter, when nothing could be gained.
How cold it was then, to be sure! But
oh! what fun when, with wooden sabots
on their feet and their sheepskins wrapped
tightly round them, they clattered along
the little frozen pathway, which had been
cut through the snow, to the dear old
church!

However, those happy days could not, and did not, last long. With all the best will in the world, the *bonne maman* could not find enough soup to fill the three young mouths which had come to her. So it happened that when Cousin Louis astonished the whole village by saying he meant to 'cross the sea' and seek his fortune in rich England, and asked if Pierre might go with him, the latter was too brave, and felt himself too much of a man, to refuse.

It is true that his heart ached sorely at the thought of going away; and that night after night he cried himself to sleep, but that was in the dark, when nobody saw or heard him. In the daytime he felt of so much importance, for all the village spoke of the wonderful journey before them, and of the fortune they would make. For had not Cousin Louis heard again and again, from the friend who was valet to an English 'milord,' how rich 'les

Anglais' were, and how they threw about
their silver and even their gold ?

Why, had not Monsieur le Curé, himself, one day called him into his little
room, and taking down a large book from
a shelf, read to him about that rich, rich
island, where the people, although so
proud and cold, were honourable and
truth-loving? He had even showed him
pictures of them. The men dressed in
large plaid coats and trousers, and the
ladies in gay shawls, their hair done in
straight curls and their large front teeth
projecting so oddly.

Little Pierre looked at them, wondering
vaguely if his teeth would ever grow like
that, while Monsieur le Curé went on to
explain to him all about the long journey
before him—how he would not only have
to travel by train, but cross the sea in a
large ship.

It had all sounded very strange and
rather awful to him then ; but it was

over now. Cousin Louis' friend, who
was in Paris at the time, had helped them
a great deal, and had told another friend
to meet them when they landed from the
ship.

England was not quite so wonderful as
he had imagined; to be sure the people
spoke very curiously, and it was a long
time before he could make out one word
they said; but he was now beginning to
understand and to be understood. Then
he discovered that all the women had not
long curls and large teeth. The English
'milords' (or what Pierre supposed to be
'milords') did not pull handfuls of gold
and silver out of the pockets of big-
checked trousers, and everyone did not
live upon roast beef! No; indeed, he had
often felt cold and wet and hungry in this
rich island, and had longed for the little
home in Auvergne.

Still, on the whole, Pierre had been very
brave and good. One thing he had never

forgotten, and that was to kneel down
night and morning and say the little
prayer Monsieur le Curé had taught him;
it always seemed to him, then, as if he
were quite near to the *bonne maman,*
Henri, and little Jeanne. Just as if the
good God took them all into His arms
together, and blessed them.

Cousin Louis, who was quick and strong,
had soon been employed as porter in an
hotel, where French people often came;
and when Pierre was bigger, and knew his
way better about the large city, he was to
go there as errand boy; in the meantime
he had sold matches, and got on pretty
well, for he had even been able to save up
a little money—three francs, which he was
hoping to send the *bonne maman* as her
étrennes; that is what little Pierre called
a New Year's present to his grannie.

But if everything has been going on so
well, you will ask why Pierre now looks so
sad and weary? Why does he not offer

his matches for sale? he has only taken twopence to-day, and has a whole trayful of boxes left.

Unfortunately things had not been going on so well lately. About a fortnight ago poor Cousin Louis had slipped down on the pavement and sprained his ankle so badly, that he had not been able to do any work since; all his small savings and Pierre's daily earnings had barely sufficed to keep them; and now, to add to the misfortune, the rent for their little garret must be paid, and Pierre's little nest-egg must pay it!

So, after all, poor grannie would have to go without her New Year's gift! Then to-day everyone had been in such a hurry, so full of business, that at last the poor little match-boy, after being first pushed here and then jostled there, had crouched down weary and dispirited upon the steps of the big, gloomy house.

He felt so sad and lonely, so full of pity

for himself, and the more he pitied himself the sadder he grew. We all know that nothing makes our courage and strength melt away more than self-pity does. It is astonishing how much lighter our own troubles become, if we think of the greater sufferings of others. Pierre was forgetting to do this now. He only remembered what a lonely, ill-used little boy he was, and so his bright hopefulness and courage began to melt away very fast indeed ; next, the tears began to gather in the dark eyes, then they rolled slowly down the sallow little cheeks, and fell plash, plash upon the gay match-boxes.

At the same moment something fell upon his hand—something so soft, and light, and damp, that he looked down quickly. It was a large white snowflake —then came another, and yet another.

The busy passers-by pulled up the collars of their coats, and hurried along quicker than ever, muttering that the

2

snowstorm had come at last, and would prove a heavy one. Then little Pierre looked up, but he smiled through his tears at the softly falling flakes, for they meant more than a coming storm to him. They were the first he had seen since he left his dear Auvergne, and were so many white-winged messengers whispering of the old home, and bidding him take heart.

'Here! my little man! any lights left?' asked a cheerful voice as a gentleman stopped for a moment before the little figure, which instantly sprang up. 'Why, a whole trayful, I declare! Not done much business to-day, eh! Well, here's something to make up for it! Get home sharp, my lad, and have a happy Christmas!'

With a kindly nod the speaker passed on, and something fell with a clink among the match-boxes.

A large piece of silver! Could it be possible? Pierre took it in his hand, turning it over with surprised delight. Happy? Of course he would be happy now, for here was money for the rent, and grannie would have her New Year's gift after all!

A happy Christmas! With beaming eyes the child once more gazed up into the now swiftly falling snow, for he guessed that it was falling just as softly and silently round the dear old home. How pure and beautiful everything would look to-morrow for the feast! It almost seemed to him as if the snowflakes were repeating to him that 'sweet story of old,' which the *bonne maman* had so often told them on Christmas Eve. The story of that wondrous night long years ago, when a little child had been born in a manger amidst the snow and ice—a little child whose baby hands were filled with gifts of love and pardon for all mankind!

Then she would go on to tell them that they must all try and make a fit home in their little hearts for the Infant Saviour, Whose delight is to be with the children of men—how they must cleanse them by sorrow for past faults, warm them with love and charity, and make them bright and pretty with good resolutions and resolves. Then they would all kneel down, and say together their night prayers. They would think of and pray for the absent Pierre, as each one in turn said reverently: 'Sweet Infant Jesus, make me a child like Thee!'

'Ah! he had not been preparing his heart for the coming Feast,' he thought sadly. Still, it was not yet too late!

At this moment a bright light, flashing up suddenly from the opposite side of the street, attracted his attention. What could it be? It was not a gas-lamp. It came—yes, surely it came from the large dark-looking church on the other side.

Pierre had often looked at this church, as he walked up and down with his matches, and wondered what it was like inside; but he had never been able to see, for the high iron gates in front were always shut and locked. Dodging his way through the omnibuses and cabs, he crossed the street. The large iron gates were open now, also the doors; so Pierre went in.

How beautiful it looked! All the pillars were twined with green leaves and shining berries, which looked so brilliant in the gas-light! Treading softly, the boy ventured partly up the aisle; then suddenly stopped. A smile of joy and wonder broke over his face as, kneeling down, he clasped his little hands.

At the extreme end of the church, in front of him, just where the light was strongest and fullest, two crimson scrolls were fixed up; something white and dazzling was sprinkled on them in the form of letters. Surely it must be snow! Pierre spelt out the words; and this is what his snowflakes told him:

'Unto us a Child is born,
Unto us a Son is given.'

Then the group of workers raised the
third and centre scroll; and 'Gloria in
excelsis Deo, in terra pax ' ('Glory to God
in the highest, on earth peace'), that
grand sweet song of the angels, broke
from their lips as they looked at the
shining letters.

And they chatted gaily of the work they
had finished, as, gathering together the
leaves and branches which were left, they
prepared to leave the church.

They did not see that which God and
the angels saw—a little boy kneeling for
a moment on the stones, forgetful of all
weariness and cold, though the freshly
fallen snow still clung about him. They
had not heard, for only God and the
angels heard, the prayer which rose from
a loving, grateful heart, and trembled on
the childish lips: 'Sweet Infant Jesus,
make me a child like Thee!'

THE SONG OF THE WIND.

THE SONG OF THE WIND.

OW bright the room looked with the lights, and plants, and flowers, and the groups of gaily dressed children dancing so merrily in time to the music !

It was like fairy-land, thought the Oleander, or that beautiful land in the south of which it so often dreamed. And that little girl with the long golden hair, and white frock floating round her like a soft cloud, was the 'Queen of the Fairies !'

Then the Oleander tried to shake its leaves and delicate pink blossoms to find out if it were really awake, and in that dull, cold land of the north to which it had been brought a tiny slip when cut from its parent tree so many years ago.

Oh yes! it was certainly wide awake; of that there could be no doubt—for at that very instant a little boy passed and roughly broke off one of its pretty flowers to throw at his cousin, who was dancing so happily with the 'Queen of the Fairies.' However, the tree soon forgot its pain in looking on at what it now knew was reality and no mere dream. What a delightful change it was, to be sure, to see so much gaiety after having been shut up so long in the quiet conservatory! Of course the Oleander had many floral companions there, although the Aloes and Camellias were nearly its only friends, as the other plants and flowers were continually coming and going. It is true that this constant change of scene gave them plenty to talk about, for they not only paid visits to the house and garden, but some of them were even invited to dine with the family from time to time, and always occupied the posts of honour —so they said—in the very centre of the table. And what wonderful stories they related of all they saw and heard! while the Oleander, who was so much bigger than any of them, knew nothing worth telling.

It had been so very young when first it was put into the conservatory, that when it was asked to entertain the company by recounting some of its experiences, it could never get beyond a confused recollection of dazzling blue sky, warm scented air, and a little child playing around the parent tree, sometimes stopping to caress its blossoms with her tiny hands. Then one day it dimly remembered that a tall maiden came, and with tears and smiles cut it (then a young and tender spray) from the parent tree. She placed cool earth and sweet damp moss around its smarting stem, and as it lay half faint with pain and fright, the little child drew near, and pressed her rosy lips for one moment to its glossy leaves. After this all seemed dark, and it remembered nothing more until it found itself in the conservatory, where it had lived ever since, and grown up.

But these memories, as I said, were so indistinct, and the Oleander spoke of them so timidly, that the Lilium Auratum would toss her saucy head, exclaiming, ' Mere childish nonsense! We cannot attend to such rubbish! Dear Miss Camellia, will you repeat once more your thrilling little romance ?'

' Oh, pray do !' the other flowers would urge; and the Oleander, silenced and ashamed, would listen to the Camellia's story, wondering sadly if it would ever have one of its own to tell.

At this moment the lace curtains in front of the open window moved gently, and a soft breeze stole in, and began fluttering among the branches of the Oleander.

' Good-evening, my little friend !' murmured the Wind. ' I have just come up from your lovely home in the south. What a pleasure to meet you so soon !'

' My home !' whispered the Tree, its

leaves trembling with excitement. 'Oh, tell me about it, dear Wind! Do you think, as the Lilium Auratum does, that all I remember about the tall maiden, the little child, the bright blue sky, and the scented air is mere childish nonsense?'

'Nonsense? No, indeed, dear Tree! Why, one of my sweetest songs is about your dear old home. Would you like to hear it?'

The Tree gently rustled its leaves for answer, and the Wind began:

'Down in the South, in that bright land where the sky is always clear and blue as a sapphire, where golden oranges, luscious figs, and clusters of purple and amber grapes ripen in the brilliant sunshine, there stood a beautiful garden. Yuccas, aloes, camellias, and roses bloomed there in wild profusion, for the gardener was not allowed to tyrannize over them by pruning their branches too closely. All the plants and flowers loved this home. The stately Magnolia-tree always wore her glossiest leaves and finest blossoms. The delicate Pepper-tree delighted to wave her feathery boughs in the warm, sweet air which blew over the garden, laden with the perfume of tuberoses and orange-blossoms, and the scarlet bloom of the Pomegranate was quite dazzling to look at. The cigale and the grasshopper made music all through the sunny day; and at night the fireflies danced merrily in and out among the olive-trees, while the little bell-frog chirped forth his silvery note.

' But amongst all the shrubs and flowers, none were so much loved by the gentle mistress of the garden as the Oleander; and of all the Oleanders, not one was so petted and cared for as the tree which grew near the fountain where the gold-fish lived. She had planted it herself when first she came to the garden, and it had always been tended by her alone. She loved to sit beside it, working and watching the little children, who each in turn played near it.

'Thus the months and seasons came and went, bringing joys and sorrows to the owner of the garden.

'The first little child had grown into a tall maiden now, and left the old home for one of her own in a far land. But before she went, she cut a tiny branch from her mother's favourite tree, that it might grow and bloom in memory of the sunny south.'

Here the Oleander trembled with joy, for it knew that its dream of the past was not 'childish nonsense' after all.

'Two other children also left the garden, but it was for a brighter one above, where the flowers and sunshine never fade. One little child still remained, who played, and laughed, and sang the livelong day.

'And the months and seasons came and went. Then suddenly a dark cloud of trouble burst over the happy garden. It broke the heart of the gentle mistress, who drooped and died; and the master's proud head was bowed with grief and shame. Poor and disgraced, he had to leave the sunny home; but he was not alone. By this time the last little child had in turn grown into a fair young maiden, and became her father's help and stay. She tried to hide her own grief, that he might always have the sunshine of her smile. She made the little home to which they went gay with flowers, and would even sing softly as she worked for their daily bread.

'How I loved to creep in through the vine that clustered round their little window, and cool her aching head, as she sat working so cheerfully at the delicate leaves and flowers she sold to the large shop in the town. Her fingers were so light, her wreaths and garlands were so well made, that they sold for more than any other person's.

'Sometimes I would manage to steal across to the corner of the room where her father sat, as if hiding away from sight. I would gently lift the white hair from his wrinkled forehead, hoping that the sweet perfume I brought him would make him raise his bowed head. But he never did. No strangers ever entered the little room, and he shrank from all his old friends, even refusing to let them know where he was. But the maiden's courage never failed. Tenderly and lovingly she cared for him, working through the sad and lonely hours, with her smile and sweet, low song.

'So the months and seasons came and went. At last they brought another change. One day when I stole in through the vine-leaves the man's chair was empty, and the maiden was quite alone!'

'And is she still quite alone?' asked the Oleander softly, as the Wind was silent for a moment.

'The last time I went into the little room, the maiden was gone, and strangers had made it their home. Can you not guess where the maiden is now?' whispered the Wind.

The little Tree trembled with a strange excitement, for see! the tall, stately mistress of the house was coming towards the window where it stood, and by her side was a maiden, oh! so sweet and fair!

'See, Ella, here is a friend from the old home waiting to welcome you! A souvenir of our mother's favourite tree!'

With smiles and tears the maiden bent down, and once more two rosy lips were pressed to the Oleander's glossy leaves.

Soon the window was closed, and the Wind went away. The lights were put out, and the music was hushed, for the merry feet were too tired to dance any more. The 'Queen of the Fairies,' who had received her mother's good-night kiss, lay sleeping, flushed and smiling in her little bed.

And the Oleander-tree? It had recognised the tall maiden and the little child it used to know so many long years ago in the beautiful garden in the south; so it had its story now, and was happy!

THE RAINDROPS.

3—2

THE RAINDROPS.

'UGLY, spiteful rain! I knew it would come to-day!' cried Mildred, as she stood at the window, her eyes full of angry tears of disappointment.

'Seems as though it likes to spoil treats,' murmured Gracie, between her sobs.

Pitter - patter, pitter - patter, splash, splash, went the rain against the nursery window in reply. And splash, splash went the tears down four sad little cheeks.

It was very hard, certainly. Aunt Kate, who lived in the country, had invited Mildred and Gracie to spend a long day, and have a good romp with their cousins

and some little friends, as it would be
Cousin Clare's birthday. As soon as they
arrived, they were to have an early dinner,
and then start for the wood, where they
would play all the afternoon; then boil
the water in the old gipsy-kettle, and have
tea under the trees.

Mamma had promised that if they were
very good, they should have a holiday and
go. For a whole week they had been
looking forward to to-day, and had worked
so hard at their lessons. Every morning
they had run the first thing to the window
to peep at the weather, and it was always
bright and sunny.

But this very day, the most important
one of all, the sky had been cloudy and
overcast. Papa, too, had looked rather
grave as he tapped the barometer in the
hall on his way out, and had said to
mamma :

'Dear me! how the glass is falling! I
hope you'll be able to go!'

They did not understand what he meant, it is true, but still they felt very anxious as they ran up to the nursery, after giving papa a good-bye kiss.

It was nearly time for them to think of putting on hats and jackets, when down came the rain in torrents, and mamma sent word to nurse that they would not be able to go to-day.

What a terrible disappointment, to be sure! Just as they were speaking, mamma came into the room, and we can easily believe that she found two wobegone and rather cross little girls crying by the window.

'I am so sorry for my pets!' said mamma. 'But we must have our holiday at home to-day; and our great treat will come soon. Aunt Kate is sure to fix another day.'

'Horrid rain!' pouted Mildred. 'It always comes when it's not wanted.'

'Perhaps it likes to make people cry,'

said little Gracie. ' Mamma, why is it so cross and unkind ?'

' I don't think it means to be that, Gracie,' replied mamma, smiling. ' Suppose I try and tell you the history of some little raindrops, where they went and what they did; and you shall decide whether they really are spiteful and cross.'

Nothing pleased Mildred and Gracie more than to hear one of mamma's tales; they always taught them so much, made them think of so many things, besides amusing them.

So they fetched two little stools, placed them close to the chair on which mamma seated herself, and in the delight of listening, they soon forgot their disappointment.

' How happy the little raindrops were the day they fell in a rattling shower on the top of the dear old mountain !

' It was the first home they could remember, and what a happy one it was, to be sure! The mountain was so kind, and had so much to show and teach them.

‘ Through sunshine, storm, and rain it was always the same—so calm and patient, protecting the small and feeble, and giving a home and nourishment even to the stiff gloomy fir-trees, whom the little raindrops thought so proud and domineering. But the mountain seemed as good to them as to the young plants and shrubs to which it lent a helping hand when they tried to climb its high steep side.

‘ The day on which the merry shower came chattering down, the drops were all so gay and full of fun that some of the most daring and mischievous of them even ventured to cluster on the branches of the solemn firs, where they lay for a few seconds sparkling with laughter. But the boughs, offended at the liberty they had taken, shook them off impatiently, and they fell to the ground, where they joined their brothers and sisters, with whom they danced joyously in a little pool, until they became such a large party that they streamed down the mountain-side.

'They trickled away one after another through the sloe-bushes and the brambles which were holding out their snowy blossoms to the hungry bees; amongst the waving grass and sweet wild thyme—stopping, however, every now and then in the midst of their mirth and frolic to cool and refresh a thirsty blade or parched-up root. Then on they went, happier than ever at having been able to do a kind action and help another.

'At length they reached the bottom of the hill, where they leapt on a large boulder which lay before them, in order to take a last peep at the kind mountain-top.

'How beautiful it looked! The wind had blown aside the fleecy clouds which had covered it like a veil, and the sun had now placed a glittering crown of gold upon its grand old head.

' " Good-bye, dear mountain," sighed the raindrops, as they splashed over the other side of the stone. " We are sorry to leave you. You make us so happy! But you taught us that we must not live all for ourselves. We are poor little things, but we'll work together, and try to remember the motto you gave us, ' Be glad and make glad!' It shall be our song as we journey along in life. Good-bye, dear mountain—good-bye!" and the last little drop dashed over the boulder stone.

' By this time they were so many in number that they became a small brook, which gurgled on over the earth and stony gravel. But it was very different here from the soft green mountain-side. No sweet young grass tempted it to pass; all was parched up and bare, so the brook found good hard work to do.

'But it worked with a will. Now we all know that "Where there's a will, there's a way." So our brooklet found, for in time it dug out a tiny bed in the gravelly soil, in which it rippled pleasantly. The little stones became bright and shining when it passed over them, and the poor thirsty ground drew strength and moisture from its kindly waters.

'As it journeyed through the dreary waste, it often felt weak and tired, and at last had scarcely the force to run; but still it struggled on, brightly and willingly giving to all it met on its way, and singing to itself the mountain's song, "Be glad, and make glad."

'Busily and happily it travelled along, never stopping to grumble or complain. By degrees the earth became soft and dark, and soon it met with grass once more. Oh, how happy it was! How it sparkled and danced on the tender turf, and burrowed its way quite close to the roots of the little green blades, which seemed like friends from the dear old home.

' " Stay ! where are you going in such a hurry ? Stop and rest a bit with me !" called out a drowsy voice.

' The little brook sprang over a branch which lay in its road, and in jumping peeped to see who spoke.

' It was a large round pool, which was lying not far off, and really seemed half-asleep, for it never troubled to move.

' "We are going through life," replied the brook, "and have so much to do that we can't stop to gossip, Mr. Pool."

' "Oh, nonsense !" rejoined the other. " If you bustle along in that absurd fashion, helping everyone you meet, you'll exhaust yourself, and be quite used up when the summer comes; and what will you do then ? No, no ; learn a lesson from me, and take care of yourself, and stay snug in your bed, and leave others to look after their own affairs. 'Everyone for himself,' is my motto, friend!"

' " The mountain told us to give all we can—to be glad, and make glad—that the good God sent us on His own bright earth to rejoice and work for Him, by helping others with a willing heart—that we must try to be happy in forgetting ourselves, and trust to God for help."

' " That's old-fashioned nonsense, my little friend! But there, I can't trouble to argue the matter. Don't bother me, that's all, when you're ruined and all dried up! Ta-ta! never mind answering me; I'm off to sleep!"

' So the brook left the selfish pool and went briskly downhill for a time, and then reached a little valley, where another young brook like a silvery ribbon was busily winding along. They agreed to join and work together, and so they became a stream which watered the valley as it passed through.

'The tall grass and slender weeds on its banks waved their thanks to it, in changing shadows which fell and played over its shining surface.

'The clouds, too, seeing the good it did, came near, and bending over it, opened their hands and filled it so full of soft splashing rain, that it grew wider and deeper the farther it went.

'It passed through meadows sprinkled with daisies and clover, where buttercups shone in golden patches. It moistened the ground, and the trunks of the trees were covered with rich green moss, in which the violet and anemone hid themselves and played with the sunbeams at hide-and-seek.

'The summer arrived, and it became very hot. The clouds gave no more rain, and the sun began to burn and scorch the land.

'The stream, however, scarcely felt the heat, for the alders and willows which grew

on its banks spread their green arms out
to shade it, and moved their boughs gently
to and fro to fan and cool its waters;
while the young twigs bent down and
kissed it and thanked it for all its care,
and nodded their green tops, as if keeping
time to the music of its song, " Be glad,
and make glad."

'The cattle came at noonday to rest on
its shady banks and quench their thirst.
And the children learned to love it, for
they soon found out that the finest forget-
me-nots and the sweetest cress could be
picked at its water's edge. So through
the long hot summer they sat and played
by its side, making daisy-chains and
wreaths of flowers which they threw to
the laughing stream.

'One day it heard the children speak of
the selfish pool. They said that its stag-
nant water had never done any good, but
slept in its bed till the thick green slime
had almost covered it. Nothing grew near

to shade or shelter it, so when the hot weather came, the sun soon dried it up. Then the farmer ordered its place to be filled up, and the pool disappeared.

'Time went by till the stream got so strong that at last it could turn the mill-wheels; then it became a river which carried barges and boats.

' Thus it sang and laboured, and flowed along till at last it drew near the sea. Then the raindrops felt that their work was done, and thought that they would now be swept away by the rolling waves.

' But why should they be afraid? They had practised the lessons which the mountain had taught them in the old home far away, "To forget themselves in their thoughtfulness for others—to be glad, and make glad—and thus to praise and serve the good God."

' Nearer and nearer they came to the sea. They could hear its loud wild roar!

Another moment and they will be swallowed up!—but no!

'The sun sent down his strong bright rays, and drew up the raindrops in a vapoury mist which floated on for a while, then sank till it lay in a soft grey cloud round the dear old mountain-top!'

'Kind little raindrops! I'm glad they reached home again!' said Gracie. 'Ah, mamma, what a lot they did! and I know you mean that we must try and be like them.'

'But how can we, I wonder?' exclaimed Mildred.

'Be glad, and make glad!' replied mamma, smiling. 'Begin with little things at home, as the raindrops did on the mountain. If you make up your minds to try, you will find out so many ways. Be bright, smiling little raindrops to papa and mamma, doing all they ask and wish. Be kind and patient with baby,

and see how you can amuse and help
your little friends. If my little girls do
this, and try to forget themselves, they
will grow into the happy stream.'

' We were sulky Mr. Pools this morning,
mamma,' said Mildred sorrowfully. ' But
we'll begin and try to be drops of rain,
won't we, Gracie ?'

Gracie nodded her head gravely.
Then drawing closer to mamma, asked :

' Must we go down to the big sea ?'

'We all go to it, Gracie ! But if my
darlings are good, they will rise up far
higher than the clouds of mist ; for our
Father in heaven, Whom they will have
loved and served, will call them to a home
far brighter than the mountain-top ! But
see, the rain is nearly over now, and I
really think we shall have a little walk together this afternoon ! And another day,
I dare say, the sunbeam will tell us a little
story !'

THE SUNBEAM'S STORY.

THE SUNBEAM'S STORY.

THE little sunbeam had been up several hours, darting about hither and thither, when it caught sight of a large tempting window. On the sill were pots of flowers, over which it danced for a second or two.

Now, if the truth must be told, our beam was rather an inquisitive little fellow, fond of pushing its way into all kinds of odd nooks and corners. So, not content with seeing the outside of the window, it suddenly sprang from the leaves of the plants through the laths of the Venetian blinds, and into the room beyond, without stopping to apologize for its unlooked-for visit, or to say, ' By your leave !'

It was a nursery, the little sunbeam saw at a glance, and a very comfortable one too. A bright flowery carpet covered the floor, pictures hung on the walls, and toys of all kinds were strewn about.

Close to the window, trying to work, sat nurse. But it was not an easy matter, for the blinds, as we have said, were down, so the room was by no means lightsome.

Our friend the beam looked round for the child, or children, who ought to have been playing about. It began to think that there were none, when the cloth, which was drawn down to the ground on the side of the table next to the window, moved slightly, and in a moment the sunbeam slipped under, determined to find out what was going on there.

'I don't want any light! I won't have it, nurse! Send it away!' screamed a peevish voice.

'It's only a little sunbeam, Miss Sophie, that's slipped through the blind.'

'Send it away, I say! I don't want the ugly thing! I will have it dark!'

The sunbeam seemed to be shaking with laughter, for it quivered all over the cross little face, and Sophie screamed louder than ever.

'Let down the blind, nurse! I *will* have it down! The horrid sun is spoiling my plague of Egypt!'

'The blind is down, darling. If it's turned darker I can't see to work.'

'I don't care! I want to play at the ninth plague of Egypt Aunt Rachel told me about, and I *will* have it dark!'

Here Sophie dragged the tablecloth angrily, and down it came! Clatter, clatter, fell nurse's work-basket and a large box of bricks; and there, under the table, sat the crossest, ugliest little girl the sunbeam had ever shone upon.

From her wide-open mouth came dismal howls, her poor eyes were so screwed up

that nothing could be seen of them, and
her heels were noisily kicking the floor.

Nurse jumped up and tried to pacify
her, but she still cried out :

'Nasty sun! It shall go away! I'll
tell mamma you won't make it dark, and
let me play!'

'Hush, my pet! hush! You'll make
yourself ill!' coaxed nurse. 'See! I'll
shut the shutters, and it will be quite
night.'

And bang went the heavy wooden
shutters on the little sunbeam. It tried
hard to discover a chink through which
it could peep in and see the game, but no
chink was to be found. So, disappointed
and pained at the rebuff it had received,
it went off and left spoilt Sophie and her
nurse to enjoy the plague of darkness
alone.

This visit had so subdued the beam,
that it had not the heart to shine again
for some time. However, when next it

came out, it played on the sooty chimneys
and grimy roof of a house in a dull, narrow
court.

Down below could be heard the sound
of children laughing, crying, romping, and
fighting. Poor little things! how dirty
and dreary their playground was! So
different from peevish Sophie's pretty
nursery! The sunbeam longed to slip
down in their midst, to have a merry
game, and whisper to them of the glad,
bright things it knew. But it was so high
up, that as it danced down the smoky
chimney-pot, it could only leap through
the garret window of the opposite house.

Such a poor, broken window it was;
all the glass was either cracked or mended
with pieces of paper and rag. But the
beam popped through an upper pane, and
into the garret it went on a voyage of dis-
covery.'

It was a tiny room, with a low, sloping
ceiling and bare, white-washed walls, which

were all discoloured. The floor, though
worm-eaten and poor, was swept as clean
as the old stump of a broom in the corner
could make it. The scanty furniture told
a tale of want and poverty. But the sunbeam did not stop to moralize or examine;
it sprang on to a bed which was opposite
the window, where it was greeted with a
faint cry of delight.

On this bed was the only occupant of
the room, a little boy, thin and wasted by
suffering.

The black lines round the large blue
eyes spoke of days and nights of sleep-
lessness and pain; and despite his efforts
to restrain them, tears of weariness were
stealing down his pale, hollow cheeks just
as the sunbeam entered with its cheery
ray.

Poor little fellow! He was tired out
with the feverish, wakeful night, and the
hard bed did not ease or rest him.

The time was passing so slowly, and

he knew that he could not expect Martha
to return for another hour at least. Dear,
kind Martha! she had always a loving
smile and word for her little brother.

When she went out to work this morning, she had placed by his side a small
bunch of violets in an old broken bottle
to keep him company. She had found
the flowers on her way home last night,
and the bottle she had picked up from the
heap of rubbish at the entrance of the
court.

The violets had been crushed and faded
when she brought them in, but they had
revived in water; and as little Tom bent
down and took them up, the sweet scent
seemed trying to cool and refresh him.

It was a moment after this that the
beam appeared, and was greeted with a
cry of joy.

Sunshine and flowers! What a lucky
boy he was! Surely he ought to be happy,
thought the child.

He stretched out his thin, white hand, and tried to grasp the merry beam, which shone now on him, and now on the pretty flowers he held towards it.

It seemed to speak to him of the pleasant country Martha often talked about, where they used to live years ago, when mother and father were alive, but which he had quite forgotten.

He tried to picture it to himself as she had sometimes described it, in the glad spring-time—the lanes with their hedges of may and twining briony; the violets and pale primroses peeping from beneath their leaves; the sloping meadows, dotted with delicate cuckoo flowers, wild snow-drops, and nodding cowslips. And country children really ran about in the midst of such sweet treasures ! The child sighed as he thought of the hot close court where his days were passed.

But as he looked again at the soft bright beam, and breathed in the perfume of his flowers, it made him think also of the quiet chats he sometimes had with Martha in the evening when her work was done, or when he felt very tired, and the pain was almost more than he could bear.

At such times she would console him by repeating the words she loved so much, that 'the sufferings of the present time are not worthy to be compared with the glory to come;' and then she would speak to him of 'the home where sorrow is unknown.'

The sunbeam now seemed like a messenger from that land of everlasting joy, whispering to him of the happiness to come. The blue eyes brightened; then by degrees the lids sank lower and lower, till, soothed by the little ray and fragrant violets, Tom fell asleep.

As he slept his face lost its weary look of pain, and the parched lips were parted in a smile. For he dreamed of the home to which he was going soon, of that city which 'hath no need of the sun nor of the moon to shine in it, for the glory of God hath enlightened it ; and the Lamb is the light thereof;' of that city where God would wipe away all tears from his eyes, and pain and death would be no more.

Lovingly the little sunbeam glided over the sleeping child, then slowly faded. Its mission was accomplished. It had raised an aching heart above earthly pain and suffering to that dear Father in heaven Who alone can comfort and console.

THE END.

R. WASHBOURNE, PRINTER, 18 PATERNOSTER ROW, LONDON.

www.ingramcontent.com/pod-product-compliance
Lightning Source LLC
Chambersburg PA
CBHW032046090426
42733CB00030B/717

* 9 7 8 3 7 4 1 1 7 8 5 3 5 *